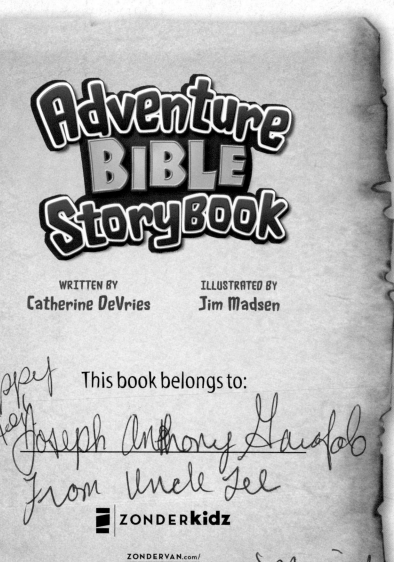

Adventure BIBLE StoryBook

WRITTEN BY
Catherine DeVries

ILLUSTRATED BY
Jim Madsen

This book belongs to:

Happy Easter *Joseph Anthony Garofalo*

From Uncle Lee

ZONDERkidz

ZONDERVAN.com/
AUTHORTRACKER
follow your favorite authors

Aunt Sandy + Mariah
We Love you!

ZONDERkidz™

Adventure Bible Storybook
© 2009 by Zondervan
Illustrations © 2009 by Jim Madsen

Requests for information should be addressed to:
Zonderkidz, Grand Rapids, Michigan 49530

Library of Congress Cataloging-in-Publication Data

Adventure Bible storybook / Catherine DeVries.

    p. cm.
    Includes bibliographical references and index.
    ISBN-13: 978-0-310-71637-2 (hardcover : alk. paper)
    Bible stories, English.
  I. DeVries, Catherine, 1968-
   BS551.3.A35 2008
  220.9'505--dc22

2007026377

Editor: Doris Rikkers
Art direction and design: Kris Nelson

Printed in China

09 10 11 12 • 5 4 3 2

To you, Brad—the love of my life—
and to our children, Bryce, Breia, and Brent.
May our home always be filled with laughter,
good books, and especially God's love.
—Catherine

To my mom and dad,
who encouraged me to
color within the lines
but forgave me when I didn't.
—Jim

Table of Contents

Old Testament

New Testament

The Adventure Begins

The big black space stretched through empty darkness. Then God created light that even the blackest night could not contain. All in one day. The very first day.

God made the trickling, bubbling, whooshing water. And up, up high, God placed the sky. God created it all in one day. The second day.

Out of the whooshing water came the land. Into the ground went roots, then sprouts appeared, and bursting buds of plants, trees, and flowers. All in one day. The third day.

Then God whirled the
sun and moon into
space. He scattered the
stars in the sky. God
made them all. In just
one day. The fourth day.

In the sea, God made fish and all kinds of creatures. In the sky, soaring birds and fluttering butterflies. God made them all in just one day. The fifth day.

What fun God had making wild animals of every kind — tall, short, furry, smooth!

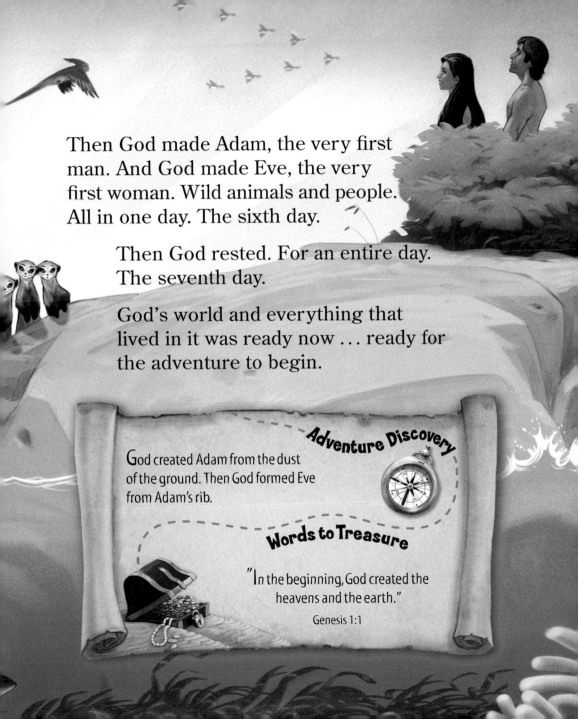

Then God made Adam, the very first man. And God made Eve, the very first woman. Wild animals and people. All in one day. The sixth day.

Then God rested. For an entire day. The seventh day.

God's world and everything that lived in it was ready now ... ready for the adventure to begin.

Adventure Discovery

God created Adam from the dust of the ground. Then God formed Eve from Adam's rib.

Words to Treasure

"In the beginning, God created the heavens and the earth."

Genesis 1:1

Adam and Eve Sin

Genesis 2:15 – 17; Genesis 3

As Eve sat on a warm rock, she felt something slide against her toes. It was a creature she had never seen before.

"What has Adam named you?" she asked.

"I am the serpent," it hissed, flicking its long tongue. "What is that delicious smell?" it asked as it slithered by.

Eve followed the serpent down a winding path. They stopped at The Tree. Many fruits hung from its branches. "It smells delicious, I agree," said Eve. "But serpent, God told us not to eat from The Tree. Any other tree is fine, but not this one."

The serpent coiled itself around a large branch. It asked, "Why wouldn't God want you to have this wonderful fruit? He's just afraid you will become like him if you eat it. Your eyes will be opened, and you will understand many things."

Eve's stomach growled. She reached toward The Tree. Just as she took a bite of fruit, Adam peeked around The Tree. "Adam, you have to try this. It is so sweet and delicious." Adam knew better, but he took a bite anyway.

Adam looked at Eve. Eve looked at the serpent. It slithered away. Something had changed. Something was not right. When Adam and Eve heard God walking in the garden, instead of running to him, they ran away.

God sent Adam and Eve out of the garden. They had disobeyed him. They had sinned. Before them was a world they did not know. They had each other, and they knew God still loved them, but their lives were changed—forever.

Adventure Discovery

After Adam and Eve left the garden, God put an angel and a flaming sword at the entrance so nobody could get back inside.

Words to Treasure

"You must not eat the fruit of the tree that is in the middle of the garden."

Genesis 3:3

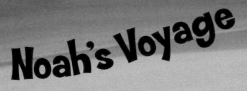

Noah's Voyage

Genesis 6 – 9

Noah swayed in his hammock, drifting in and out of sleep. The rain was coming down hard now. And the thunder sounded close. Noah could hear the squawks, oinks, woofs, moos, baa-as, and roars of all the animals in his noisy neighborhood. It wasn't easy living here.

Suddenly the ark lurched, and Noah fell out of his hammock. It was time to milk the cows anyway. Even though it was dark, Noah knew exactly where he was. He heard his wife's footsteps. Her basket of eggs clunked his back as she walked by. "Oops, sorry," she said. "Breakfast will be ready soon, if I can keep these eggs in the pan. The storm sure is strong today!"

Noah looked forward to the day when he would walk on steady ground again and see horses gallop across golden fields, monkeys leap from tree to tree, and turtles meander through the green grass.

"Thank you, God," said Noah, clasping his rough, worn hands together. "Thank you for promising to save me, my family, and these animals."

The first beams of morning light streamed into the dark ark. A dove flew down from the rafters and perched on a windowsill. Soon the dove would fly out that window and never come back. Because it would find land . . . and so would the ark. And a new adventure in God's world would begin.

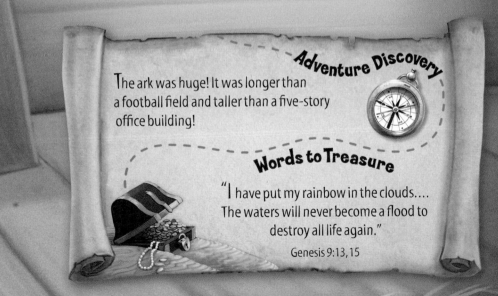

Adventure Discovery

The ark was huge! It was longer than a football field and taller than a five-story office building!

Words to Treasure

"I have put my rainbow in the clouds.... The waters will never become a flood to destroy all life again."

Genesis 9:13, 15

God's Promise to Abram

Genesis 15

Abram (soon to be known as Abraham) looked across the valley. The stars above glittered like jewels in a treasure chest. A booming voice echoed through the valley, "Abram ... Abram."

Abram knew who it was.

"Yes, Lord," he answered.

"Count the stars in the sky. Tell me how many there are."

Abram laughed. "Lord, you know
I am too old to see that far.
Besides, there are too many
stars to count!"

"So shall your offspring be!"
God said.

"How can this be?" Abram asked. "I don't have any children, and I'm an old man."

God told Abram that his wife, Sarai (soon to be known as Sarah), would have a baby boy. Abram imagined holding his baby and tickling his little cheek. It took Abram a minute to understand. But he believed because God said it would be so.

God promised to watch over Abram and his family's families after him. This promise, or covenant, was part of a long, long friendship God would keep with his special, chosen people. If they trusted in him, God would always love and protect them. He would lead them on whatever journeys they would take and show them what to do through every adventure.

Adventure Discovery

When little Isaac was born, Abram was 100 years old and Sarai was 90!

Words to Treasure

On that day the Lord made a covenant with Abram.

Genesis 15:18

Joseph and the Slave Traders

Genesis 37 – 50

In less than a day, Joseph's life had gone from
terrific to terrible. He looked down at his
hands tied in ropes. Stinging sweat dripped
into his eyes. All he could see was the cloud of
dust that the animals kicked into the air.

Joseph's brothers had grown tired of him. They
were tired of Joseph being their dad's favorite.
And they were tired of hearing about Joseph's
dreams—especially the ones about them bowing
down to him. They took matters into their own
hands. They ripped off his robe—a special
present from Dad—and threw Joseph into a
deep hole.

Joseph was trapped
for hours before he
heard something hit
the ground — a rope.
"At last, they've come
back," he sighed with
relief.

But as he climbed out of the hole, Joseph didn't see his brothers. Instead he found himself face-to-face with slave traders. They tied his hands up and led him away from his home.

Joseph shut his eyes for a moment and thought, My dreams have turned into a nightmare. Little did Joseph know that God would use this hard time in his life as a way to save thousands and thousands of people from going hungry … including his brothers. Many years later, they would all be together again as one family to face new adventures in the land of Egypt.

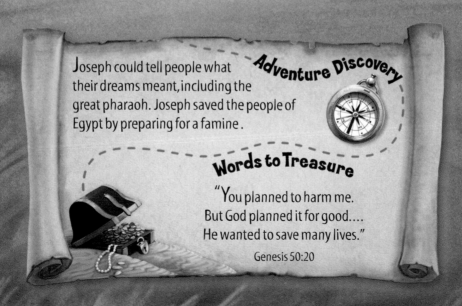

Adventure Discovery

Joseph could tell people what their dreams meant, including the great pharaoh. Joseph saved the people of Egypt by preparing for a famine.

Words to Treasure

"You planned to harm me. But God planned it for good.… He wanted to save many lives."
Genesis 50:20

Baby Moses

Exodus 2: 1–10

Miriam scanned the river. "So far, so good,"
she said as she lifted the basket out of the river.
She wanted to make sure her baby brother was
okay. I'd better be careful. No one can see I'm

here, she reminded herself. She put the basket
back into the water, and carefully parted the
reeds and went back to her hiding place.

Suddenly she heard the baby's cry. She tried to catch up with the basket, but it was now bobbing up and down in the deepest part of the river. A tiny little arm reached out.

Miriam was scared. If she went to him, someone would surely see her. Putting the baby in the river was the only way her family thought they could save him. He cried again … and again.

Just then Miriam spotted a beautiful lady at the edge of the river. Miriam crouched down out of sight and peered through the tall grass. The lady, a princess, called to her servant and pointed to the basket. The servant waded out in the river and brought the basket to shore.

Miriam watched for a minute and waited. Then she waded toward the women, pushing through the reeds toward the basket that held her baby brother.

The princess reached into the basket and
gently picked up the baby. "There, there," she
cooed. "It's all right now. Shush, my little one."

Miriam approached the woman, her voice shaking. "I see that you have a little baby," said Miriam. "I know someone who could … who could nurse the baby for you."

The princess smiled at Miriam. "Oh, thank you, how kind. Yes, please go, bring her to me. This baby will be my son. I will name him Moses."

Miriam ran home with a smile on her face. She couldn't wait to tell her mother the wonderful news. Her precious baby brother had been saved by the princess of Egypt!

Adventure Discovery

Can you guess who nursed the baby for the princess? Yes! It was Miriam's mother (the baby's real mother).

Words to Treasure

We know that in all things God works for the good of those who love him.

Romans 8:28

The Plagues

Exodus 3; 7 – 12

Moses rested his head on his shepherd's staff.
How would this idea of God's ever work? He
had been out in the middle of nowhere watching
his sheep when God suddenly appeared in a
burning bush and told him to go back to Egypt
to free God's people. Moses didn't know what
to expect, but God told him to go.

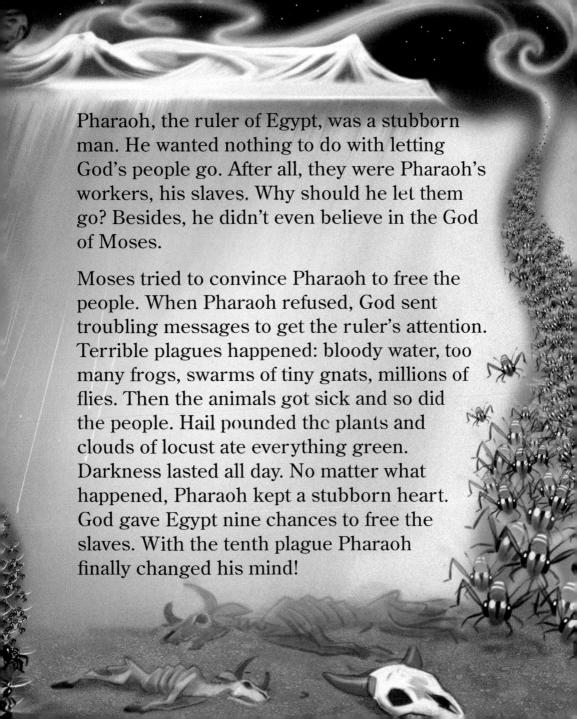

Pharaoh, the ruler of Egypt, was a stubborn man. He wanted nothing to do with letting God's people go. After all, they were Pharaoh's workers, his slaves. Why should he let them go? Besides, he didn't even believe in the God of Moses.

Moses tried to convince Pharaoh to free the people. When Pharaoh refused, God sent troubling messages to get the ruler's attention. Terrible plagues happened: bloody water, too many frogs, swarms of tiny gnats, millions of flies. Then the animals got sick and so did the people. Hail pounded the plants and clouds of locust ate everything green. Darkness lasted all day. No matter what happened, Pharaoh kept a stubborn heart. God gave Egypt nine chances to free the slaves. With the tenth plague Pharaoh finally changed his mind!

When all the firstborn sons of the Egyptians died, including the pharaoh's son, Pharaoh agreed to let God's people go.

Pharaoh had changed his mind nine times before. Would this time be different?

Adventure Discovery

Moses told God's people to put lamb's blood on their door frames so the angel of death would "pass over" their houses. This "pass over" night is still celebrated today.

Words to Treasure

The Lord says, "Let my people go."
Exodus 8:20

The Great Escape

Exodus 12–14

A long, long line of God's people walked out of Egypt toward the Red Sea. Hundreds of thousands of Hebrews were free at last!

As Moses led God's people into the desert, they thought about the long, hard years they had spent making bricks and working in the fields.

A girl hugged her doll close as she walked in
the middle of the crowd. Her mother held her
hand as they caught up with their family.

Suddenly their thoughts were interrupted. Was
that thunder? A storm on the way? It couldn't
be. There wasn't a storm cloud in the sky.

Then they saw an enormous blanket of sand rising up from the desert floor. Pharaoh's army was coming! Hundreds of soldiers in thundering chariots were following close behind!

Adventure Discovery

Pharaoh had more than 600 chariots in his army.

Words to Treasure

"Don't be afraid. Stand firm. You will see how the Lord will save you today."

Exodus 14:13

Through the Sea

Exodus 14

What would God's people do? There was nowhere to hide. And no way to outrun Pharaoh and his massive army. The Red Sea was in front of them, and Pharaoh's chariots were behind them. There was nowhere to go. They were stuck!

Moses took a deep breath.

"Just raise your staff," God told Moses. "Then I will make the water split in half, and you and my people can cross the sea on dry ground."

When Moses raised his staff, the wind blew and the water began to churn. Slowly a pathway appeared. God's people walked through the sea as the Egyptians charged closer. Just as the last of God's people stepped onto the far bank, the water tumbled across the dry path. The Egyptian army was caught in the sea. By the grace and amazing power of God, his people were free to face the great adventures God had planned for them.

Adventure Discovery

It probably took eight to twelve hours for the waters to part.

Words to Treasure

"The Lord will fight for you. Just be still."

Exodus 14:14

Food from Heaven

Exodus 16

A boy looked up into the sky. Little white puffs were falling, landing on his head, his hands, his clothes. He asked his mother, "What is it?" It looked like snow. The boy opened his mouth and caught a flake on his tongue. It didn't melt into water like snow. It tasted more like bread. The boy got up and told his friends about his discovery. Soon children were running everywhere, their mouths open wide, enjoying the snack that tasted like bread sweetened with honey.

The boy's mother didn't know what it was. Nobody had seen anything like it. But God told Moses about it and said that the people should gather up just what they needed every morning. It would be their food in the desert. They called the food from heaven "manna," which means, "what is it?"

Day after day, week after week, year after year, for forty years, the manna fell from the sky. And no one has seen anything like it ever again.

Adventure Discovery

God's people collected enough manna for one day's worth of food. On Friday they collected enough food for two days—Friday and Saturday (their day of rest).

Words to Treasure

Then the Lord spoke to Moses. He said, "I will rain down bread from heaven for you."

Exodus 16:4

Mountaintop Moment

Exodus 19 – 20; 32; 34

The wind nearly pushed Moses off the rock he was sitting on. Only Moses was allowed to be on top of the mountain. Only he was allowed to meet with God.

God's people waited at the bottom of the mountain, wondering what news Moses would bring back from God.

In a big cloud of fire, smoke, and wind, God came down to the mountaintop. God told Moses many, many things. When Moses went down the mountain and told the people what God wanted, they said, "We will do everything the Lord has told us to do."

Lightning lit up the sky and revealed a thick
cloud of smoke that made the mountain
look like it was on fire. God wrote the Ten
Commandments on two stone tablets so the
people would know the rules that would keep
them safe and free. God gave the tablets to
Moses when he went back up the mountain.

But when Moses returned to the people, they were not keeping their promise to God. They had collected all the gold in the camp, melted it, and made a statue. They were worshiping a calf made of gold instead of God! Moses was so angry that he threw down the stone tablets. They broke into pieces.

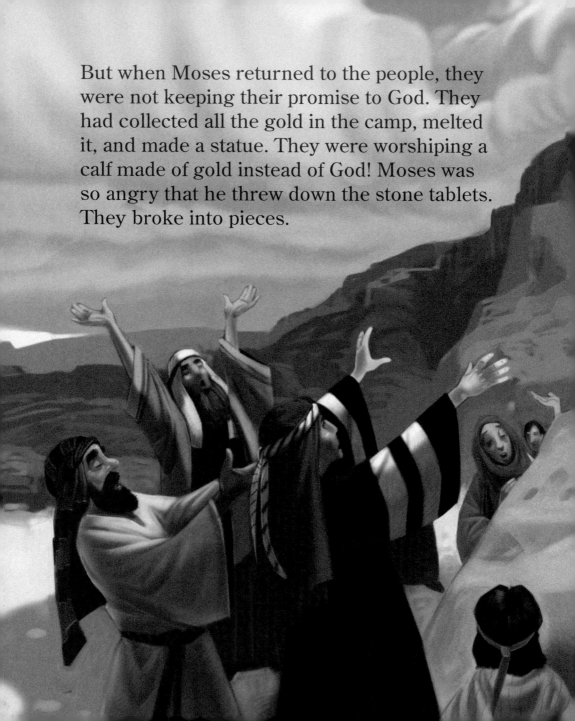

Later God wrote the Ten Commandments on two new stone tablets. These tablets were kept safe inside the ark of the covenant. (Go to page 101 for more on the ark of the covenant.)

Moses realized that his life was full of adventure—few people had ever talked to God like he had!

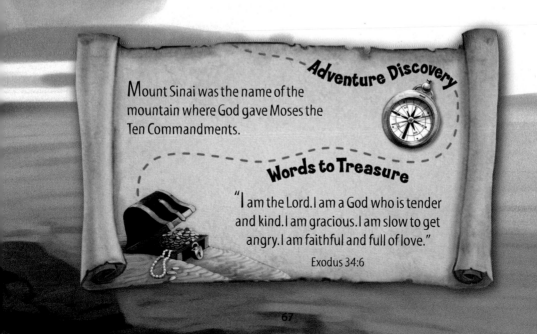

Adventure Discovery

Mount Sinai was the name of the mountain where God gave Moses the Ten Commandments.

Words to Treasure

"I am the Lord. I am a God who is tender and kind. I am gracious. I am slow to get angry. I am faithful and full of love."

Exodus 34:6

Oh No, It's Jericho!

Joshua 6

Joshua, the new leader of God's people, stood on a hilltop and shielded his eyes from the bright sun. He and God's people were at the edge of the desert looking at a lush, green valley with winding rivers, flourishing trees, and blossoming plants. Here was the land that God had promised: a land flowing with milk and honey. The Promised Land.

Joshua spotted something in the distance that stood between God's people and the Promised Land. It was the city of Jericho.

Jericho was surrounded by a huge, strong wall. A giant, solid gate made of wood and iron stayed tightly closed. No one went in. No one went out. How would God's people ever make it to the Promised Land with this fortress in the way?

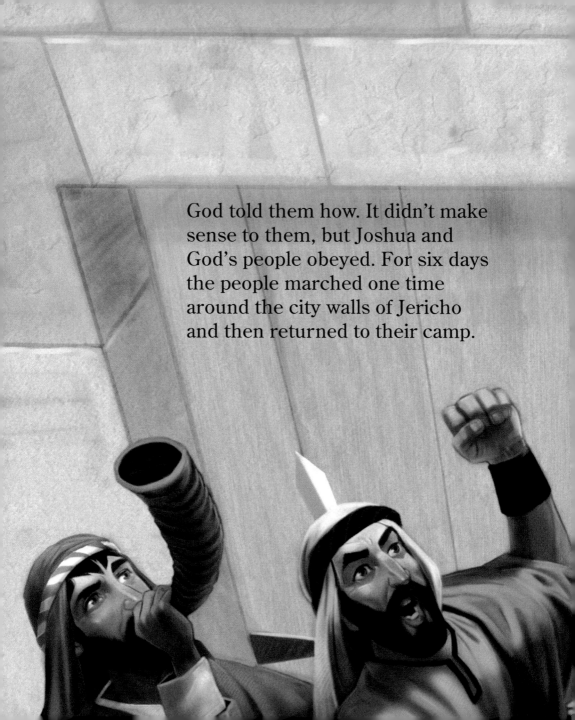

God told them how. It didn't make sense to them, but Joshua and God's people obeyed. For six days the people marched one time around the city walls of Jericho and then returned to their camp.

On the seventh day, the people marched around the city walls seven times. The final time around the city, the priests blew their trumpets. Then Joshua lifted his sword and signaled God's people. Together they yelled at the top of their lungs.

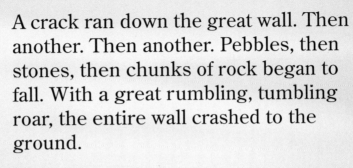

A crack ran down the great wall. Then another. Then another. Pebbles, then stones, then chunks of rock began to fall. With a great rumbling, tumbling roar, the entire wall crashed to the ground.

God's people won the battle over Jericho and were able to enter the Promised Land. God's dream for his people had come true!

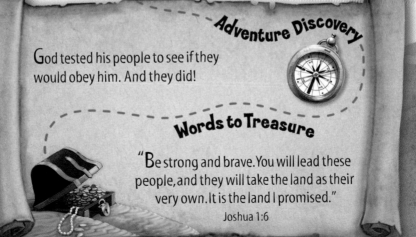

Adventure Discovery

God tested his people to see if they would obey him. And they did!

Words to Treasure

"Be strong and brave. You will lead these people, and they will take the land as their very own. It is the land I promised."

Joshua 1:6

Gideon Gets Going

Judges 7

In the middle of the night Gideon motioned for the men to get into position around the enemy's camp. As he waited, Gideon thought about how God had led him to where he now stood.

Gideon had never been a good soldier. A soldier always took orders. But not Gideon. When God gave Gideon his orders, Gideon questioned them. He wanted to be sure he heard God right. He wanted proof. And every time, God had provided the proof Gideon needed to get going.

Ever since they entered the Promised Land,
God's people had been fighting their enemies.
Now Gideon's small army was on the brink of
another battle, about to attempt the impossible.

His band of 300 men faced thousands and thousands of trained soldiers! But Gideon's group had something the enemy didn't— God was on their side.

When the Israelites were in position around the enemy camp, Gideon gave the signal. Suddenly a loud crashing sound shattered the quiet night. The enemy jolted awake and looked out from their tents. Torches of light surrounded their camp. The sound of breaking pots and shouting men struck them with terror. The enemy army was certain that their camp was surrounded by thousands of soldiers and that it was only a matter of time before they would be defeated. They scrambled for their weapons and their armor but got confused in the darkness. They started fighting each other instead of Gideon's army.

Gideon raised his sword and all the men in his army roared, "A sword for the Lord and for Gideon!"

That night God and his people won the battle!

Gideon's army took the enemy army by surprise. They used confusion to their advantage.

Adventure Discovery

Words to Treasure

"A sword for the Lord and for Gideon!"

Judges 7:20

Samson's Secret

Judges 13 – 16

Samson's muscles rippled
through his arms and chest.
He pushed with all his might on
the two tall pillars that held up
the building.

Samson had always been strong. When he was born, an angel told his parents that he would be set apart to God and that he was never supposed to cut his hair. As long as his hair was not cut, he would have incredible strength. This was a secret he knew he shouldn't tell anyone.

As he got older, Samson's hair grew long, and he became very powerful. He tore apart a lion with his bare hands. He defeated a thousand men without a sword or spear, just a jawbone from a donkey. And he tore off a huge city gate and carried it all the way to the top of a hill! Everyone knew about Samson's strength.

Samson led the people of Israel for twenty years. But Samson did not always follow the rules. And he made friends with the wrong people.

One time he fell in love with a crafty woman named Delilah. She made Samson tell her the secret of his strength. What a big mistake!

In no time, Delilah told Samson's secret to his enemies, the Philistines. While Samson slept, they cut his hair. Then they blinded him and put him in jail. Samson's power had left him, and he was like any other man. But his hair began to grow, and so did his strength.

Now Samson stood in front of over 3,000 Philistines who came to worship their false god and to make fun of Samson. The columns of the temple began to sway. Samson asked God to make him strong one last time. He wanted to destroy this temple full of evil Philistines who did not believe in the one true God.

Suddenly the columns gave way and the temple tumbled to the ground in a pile of rubble. All the people, including Samson, were destroyed.

Adventure Discovery

Samson killed more people when he died than when he was alive.

Words to Treasure

[Samson] said, "Lord and King, show me that you still have concern for me. God, please make me strong just one more time."

Judges 16:28

Boy Versus Giant

1 Samuel 17

They stood in front of their armies ready for battle. One boy and one giant. The armies watched. The kings waited. The earth rumbled with the giant's footsteps. "I will feed you to the birds after I'm through with you," he bellowed.

The crowd watched and winced. This boy was no match for the giant they called Goliath.

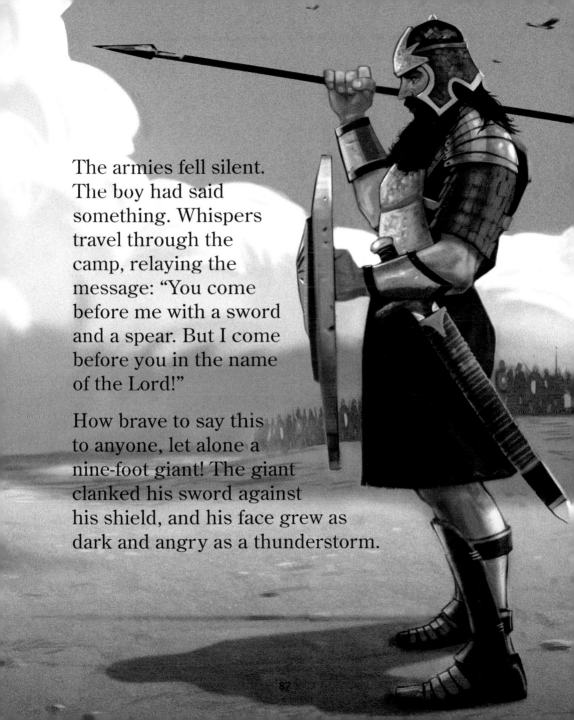

The armies fell silent. The boy had said something. Whispers travel through the camp, relaying the message: "You come before me with a sword and a spear. But I come before you in the name of the Lord!"

How brave to say this to anyone, let alone a nine-foot giant! The giant clanked his sword against his shield, and his face grew as dark and angry as a thunderstorm.

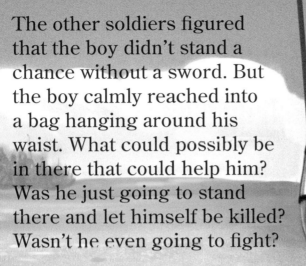

The other soldiers figured that the boy didn't stand a chance without a sword. But the boy calmly reached into a bag hanging around his waist. What could possibly be in there that could help him? Was he just going to stand there and let himself be killed? Wasn't he even going to fight?

The boy pulled out a smooth stone from the bag, loaded his slingshot, and ran toward the giant. He whirled his sling around and around, and released the stone into the air at lightning speed.

Before the giant knew what had hit him, he was on the ground. The stone hit his forehead and killed him.

David's army cheered. The battle was over. All because of this boy and his trust in God!

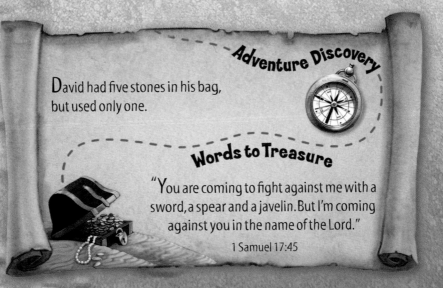

Adventure Discovery

David had five stones in his bag, but used only one.

Words to Treasure

"You are coming to fight against me with a sword, a spear and a javelin. But I'm coming against you in the name of the Lord."

1 Samuel 17:45

The Shepherd's Song

Psalm 23

Another beautiful day in the fields. The sheep were wandering nearby, nibbling tender green shoots of grass. David held a baby lamb, born a few weeks earlier, in his arms. Its wooly coat was curly and soft.

Young David loved being outdoors. He felt so close to God, the Creator of all things, when he felt the wind blowing on his face and heard the bleating chorus of his sheep. One day David felt so full of love for God that he wrote a psalm recognized even today:

Psalm 23

Psalm 23:1 The Lord is my shepherd, I shall not be in want.

Psalm 23:2 He makes me lie down in green pastures, he leads me beside quiet waters,

Psalm 23:3 he restores my soul. He guides me in paths of righteousness for his name's sake.

Psalm 23:4 Even though I walk through the valley of the shadow of death, I will fear no evil, for you are with me; your rod and your staff, they comfort me.

Psalm 23:5 You prepare a table before me in the presence of my enemies. You anoint my head with oil; my cup overflows.

Psalm 23:6 Surely goodness and love will follow me all the days of my life, and I will dwell in the house of the Lord forever.

(NIV Translation)

David wrote this song about being a shepherd before he became king.

Adventure Discovery

Words to Treasure

The Lord is my shepherd,
I shall not be in want.

Psalm 23:1 NIV

The Magnificent Temple

1 Kings 6 – 8

King Solomon stood in front of the dazzling temple. More beautiful than any other building, it glittered with gold and gleamed with fine wood. Carvings of lilies, palm trees, and pomegranates decorated the inside of the temple and the wall that surrounded it.

King Solomon spread out his hands toward heaven. He said before the whole community of Israel, "Lord, you are the God of Israel. There is no God like you in heaven above or on earth below. You keep the covenant you made with us. You show us your love. You do that when we follow you with all our hearts."

As he stood in front of the people, Solomon thought about the past seven years and the hard work of building the grand temple. He had followed the directions from his father, King David.

Inside the magnificent temple, Solomon
built a special room called the Most Holy
Place. The ark of the covenant of the Lord
would stay there.

Giant statues of angel-like creatures called
cherubim surrounded the ark. Their
golden wings glistened and reached from
wall to wall.

Now with the temple completed, Solomon looked across the enormous crowd of people who had come to celebrate. They watched as the priests brought the ark of the Lord's covenant to its place in the Most Holy Place of the temple. They put it under the wings of the cherubim. And the glory of the Lord filled his temple like a cloud.

Then Solomon said, "Lord, you have said you would live in a dark cloud. As you can see, I've built a beautiful temple for you. You can live in it forever." The whole community of Israel stood at the entrance to the temple as the king turned around and gave them his blessing.

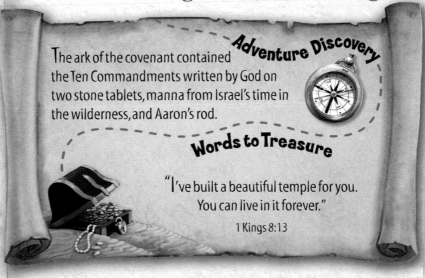

Adventure Discovery

The ark of the covenant contained the Ten Commandments written by God on two stone tablets, manna from Israel's time in the wilderness, and Aaron's rod.

Words to Treasure

"I've built a beautiful temple for you. You can live in it forever."

1 Kings 8:13

Words of Wisdom

Proverbs 1–22

King Solomon, known for his extraordinary God-given wisdom, delivered important counsel that can be found in the book of Proverbs. Proverbs teach wisdom and encourage us to do what is right, honest, and fair.

Solomon's Wise Words

Proverbs 1:7 If you really want to gain knowledge, you must begin by having respect for the Lord. But foolish people hate wisdom and training.

Proverbs 1:10 If sinners tempt you, don't give in to them.

Proverbs 2:3 Call out for the ability to be wise. Cry out for understanding.

Proverbs 2:4 Look for [wisdom] as you would look for silver. Search for it as you would search for hidden treasure.

Proverbs 3:3 Don't let love and truth ever leave you. Tie them around your neck. Write them on the tablet of your heart.

Proverbs 3:5 Trust in the Lord with all your heart. Do not depend on your own understanding.

Proverbs 3:25 Don't be terrified by sudden trouble. Don't be afraid when sinners are destroyed.

Proverbs 3:26 The Lord is the one you will trust in.

Proverbs 10:12 Hate stirs up fights. But love erases all sins by forgiving them.

Proverbs 12:25 Worry makes a man's heart heavy. But a kind word cheers him up.

Proverbs 12:26 Godly people are careful about the friends they choose. But the way of sinners leads them down the wrong path.

Proverbs 15:1 A gentle answer turns anger away. But mean words stir up anger.

Proverbs 15:18 A man who burns with anger stirs up fights. But a person who is patient calms things down.

Proverbs 16:3 Commit to the Lord everything you do. Then your plans will succeed.

Proverbs 19:17 Anyone who is kind to poor people lends to the Lord. God will reward him for what he has done.

Proverbs 22:9 Anyone who gives freely will be blessed. That's because he shares his food with those who are poor.

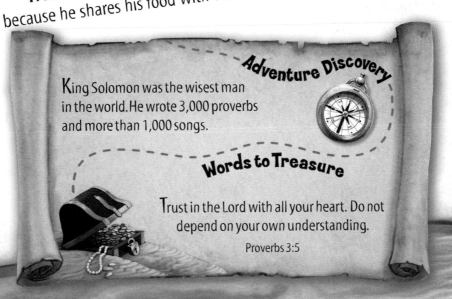

Adventure Discovery

King Solomon was the wisest man in the world. He wrote 3,000 proverbs and more than 1,000 songs.

Words to Treasure

Trust in the Lord with all your heart. Do not depend on your own understanding.

Proverbs 3:5

Elijah's Whirlwind

1 Kings 18 – 19; 2 Kings 2

Elijah's pure white beard brushed against his chest. His life had been filled with adventure. He had won a dramatic contest to see if God or Baal was the true God. He had escaped from Queen Jezebel, the wicked queen of Israel. He had survived in the desert because God had provided meat and bread every day. God had been with him through it all.

Now, on this day, Elijah would be taken to heaven. His helper, Elisha, insisted on walking with him. "I won't leave you," he said. When they reached the Jordan River, the prophets witnessed an amazing miracle. Elijah hit the water with his coat, and the river parted in two so they could cross it on dry ground.

Old Elijah turned to his friend and asked, "What can I do for you before I'm taken away from you?"

Elisha replied, "Please give me a double share of your spirit."

"If you see me taken from you," Elijah replied, "you will have your wish."

Suddenly a chariot and horses of fire appeared. A whirlwind lifted Elijah off the ground in a great gust of wind that lifted him up to heaven. As quickly as they had arrived, the blazing chariot and horses left with Elijah.

Elisha picked up Elijah's coat, which had been left behind. With it he hit the Jordan River, and the water parted! Elisha crossed to the other side, ready to face the adventures God had in store for him.

Adventure Discovery

Elijah is only one of two people who have gone to heaven without dying. If you want to find out who the other person is, open your Bible to Genesis 5:24.

Words to Treasure

Elijah went up to heaven in a strong wind.

2 Kings 2:11

Naaman's Journey

2 Kings 5

Naaman stood next to the window and gazed at the beautiful sunset. His uniform hung in the corner, along with his armor and powerful sword. As a commander in the army he had won many battles. But there was one battle he could not win — his battle with leprosy.

Naaman heard a rustling sound behind him. It was his wife's servant, bringing them supper. As she laid out the food, she smiled and said, "I know someone who can heal you."

Naaman dropped his spoon. "How can this be?" he replied. "I've been to the best doctors, and they say nothing can be done for me."

The servant girl answered, "There is a prophet in Israel named Elisha. He can heal you."

With hope Naaman went to see the prophet of God, Elisha. Naaman knocked, but no one came to the door. Not even after he made it clear that he was an important commander.

Finally a servant arrived with a message from Elisha: Go into the Jordan River and dip in it seven times. Then you will be healed.

Naaman grew angry. Elisha hadn't even come out to see him, and now he was instructed to go swimming in a stinky river? "Ridiculous," he grumbled as he walked away. But the men who were with Naaman pleaded with him to stay ... and try it.

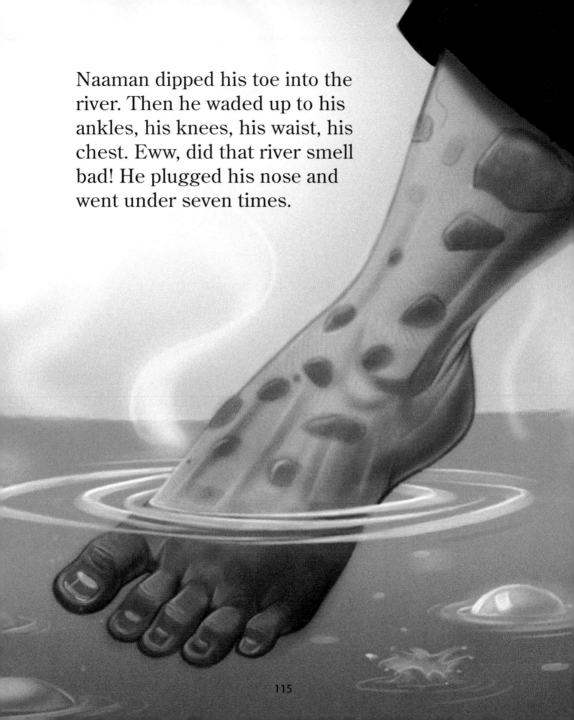

Naaman dipped his toe into the river. Then he waded up to his ankles, his knees, his waist, his chest. Eww, did that river smell bad! He plugged his nose and went under seven times.

When he finished, he headed for shore, relieved
that he could get out of that water and change
into dry clothes. But before he got out, his
servants gasped. What was wrong? Naaman
looked at his hands. He touched his face. He
rubbed one foot on top of the other. His skin was
silky and, oh, so smooth! His leprosy was gone.
He was cured!

Adventure Discovery

Naaman was proud. He was a very important person. It was hard for him to follow the instructions to jump into the dirty Jordon River.

Words to Treasure

"Now I know that there is no God anywhere in the whole world except in Israel."

2 Kings 5:15

Esther and the King

Esther 2 – 10

Esther twirled her dress in a perfect circle and smiled at the king. Of all the women in the beauty contest, the king liked Esther the best. So Esther became the queen.

Esther lived in the royal palace and had many servants and attendants to take care of her. Still she kept in close touch with her beloved, trusted cousin, Mordecai.

One day Esther's friends delivered a message from Mordecai—they had worried looks on their faces.

"What's wrong?" Esther asked.

They looked into her eyes. "Mordecai wants you to know that there is trouble ahead."

"Tell me more," she said.

"There's a plot from the palace to kill all the Jews!" one of her friends blurted out.

Esther gasped. How could this be? This was terrible news not only for the Jewish people, but also for the queen. She was Jewish too, but no one in the palace knew that. Or had someone found out?

Esther had to take action. But it was against the rules for her to go directly to the king for her requests. Mordecai encouraged her to speak to the king anyway. "Perhaps you were made queen for such a time as this," he said.

Even though she could get into a lot of trouble, Esther risked going before the king. "Oh, please, my dear king," she said. "Please do not kill the Jews. For I am a Jew. And if you kill them, you must also kill me!"

At first the king was confused. He didn't realize he had been used to forward the plot to kill all the Jews. "Someone has tricked me!" he shouted. When the king found out who it was, he got rid of him.

Then the king appointed Mordecai as his new advisor. Through Esther and Mordecai, the Jewish people were saved!

Adventure Discovery

Esther went through one full year of beauty treatments at the palace before the king even saw her!

Words to Treasure

"Who knows? It's possible that you became queen for a time just like this."

Esther 4:14

Drooling Lions

Daniel 6

The lions paced around Daniel.
Even though the den was dark, Daniel
could see their shining eyes, circling
around him. Getting closer and closer.

Daniel fell to his knees. He lifted his hands and prayed to God, just like he did every day. He prayed, "Oh, Lord, I know you are with me. I trust you."

As he opened his eyes, Daniel searched for the eyes of the lions. But he couldn't see them. And he couldn't hear the lions' angry growl, or the sound of their tails swishing back and forth.

Instead Daniel saw something he didn't expect.
He blinked several times. There it was—over
in the corner. An angel of the Lord. The wild
beasts turned away from Daniel.

Even though it was dark, the angel who
guarded him knew right where he was.

Daniel curled up on the other side of the den and fell into a deep sleep.

When daylight streamed through the cracks in the den, the king arrived and shouted to Daniel.

Daniel woke up and said, "The Lord has saved me from the mouths of the lions!"

The king freed Daniel and told everyone in his kingdom to worship the God of Daniel—the one true God.

Adventure Discovery

No matter what, Daniel prayed to God three times every day.

Words to Treasure

"My God sent his angel. And his angel shut the mouths of the lions. They haven't hurt me at all."
Daniel 6:22

Fish Food

Jonah 1 – 4

Jonah picked a fishbone out of his hair and looked around. He couldn't see anything, but he could feel the clumps of seaweed sloshing past him in the water.

It had all happened so fast. One minute he was swimming as hard as he could. The next he was eyeball-to-eyeball with a gigantic fish.

A rush of water forced him past tongue and teeth, and down the creature's throat to the place he was now—inside the belly of this great big fish. Jonah began to wonder if he would get out alive.

He thought back to when God had told him to go the city of Nineveh. God wanted his prophet to urge the people there to change their ways from bad to good.

Instead Jonah boarded a ship and traveled in the opposite direction across the sea. Then a terrible storm blew in. The sailors were scared, but Jonah knew God had sent the storm. Jonah told the men to throw him overboard. When they did, the storm stopped. Instantly.

While inside the fish, Jonah prayed to God for three days. He told God he was very sorry for not obeying, for not going to Nineveh.

Suddenly Jonah was tossed in the churning belly of the fish. The water sloshed higher and higher. After a loud gurgle, Jonah came out the same way he had gone down three days before — over the tongue, past the teeth, and out the mouth of the giant fish.

Daylight blinded him for a moment, but finally, surprisingly, he was on solid ground. Jonah got up, wiped himself off. When God told Jonah to go to Nineveh a second time, he obeyed. He faced a new adventure. He had to give the people a message from God.

Adventure Discovery

The people of Nineveh listened to Jonah, and they turned from their bad ways.

Words to Treasure

From inside the fish Jonah prayed to the Lord his God.

Jonah 2:1

Earth Bound

Luke 2:1 – 7

The world was silent. And most everyone was fast asleep. What seemed like a normal night, with the moon and the stars shining brightly overhead, would become a night like no other.

A woman rode a donkey into Bethlehem. Her tummy was huge. Very soon she would give birth to her baby. Joseph and Mary went to every inn to see if there was any room for them to stay. But at all the doors, the people just shook their heads no. Then a door opened. A man peered out and noticed Mary.

"Looks like she needs a place to rest," he said. "You can stay in my stable out back. It's not much, but at least it's warm and dry."

Joseph pushed open the worn, wooden door and helped Mary down from the donkey. With great relief, she lay down on the bed of straw. Joseph ran to get some water and a few towels. And just in time …

Mary's son was born. His cries in the night echoed through the empty streets of Bethlehem.

Mary looked down at her precious baby boy. "Hello, Jesus," she whispered. She laid him down and snuggled close.

God had come to earth as a little baby. He would someday save the world.

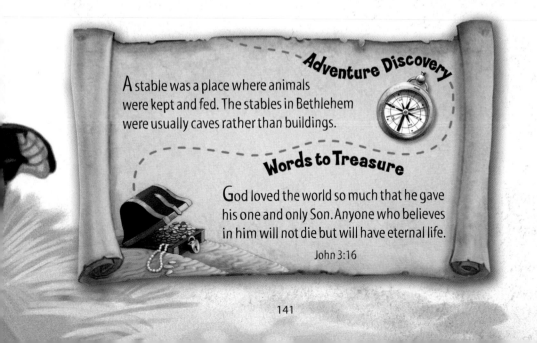

Adventure Discovery

A stable was a place where animals were kept and fed. The stables in Bethlehem were usually caves rather than buildings.

Words to Treasure

God loved the world so much that he gave his one and only Son. Anyone who believes in him will not die but will have eternal life.

John 3:16

Angels Tell the Shepherds

Luke 2:8 – 20

That same evening outside the city, shepherds gathered around a campfire and relaxed after a hard day's work in the open fields.

From out of nowhere, an angel appeared with a very important announcement: "Christ the Savior is born. Go and find him."

The shepherds looked up and heard singing. Hundreds of angels joined together in a huge choir. They sang, "May glory be given to God in the highest heaven! And may peace be given to those he is pleased with on earth!"

The shepherds forgot about the campfire and their hard day. They were mesmerized by the singing. They had never seen such sights and sounds as these.

When the angels disappeared, the shepherds hurried to the nearby town of Bethlehem.

They found baby Jesus and praised God. The Savior of the world had come!

Adventure Discovery

The Bible gives us the names of only two angels: Gabriel and Michael. But we do not know if they were in the choir of angels who sang when Jesus was born.

Words to Treasure

"Today in the town of David a Savior has been born to you. He is Christ the Lord."

Luke 2:11

Gifts from the Wise Men

Matthew 2:1 – 12

A brilliant star shone in the dark night sky.
The wise men looked at each other. They knew
what this meant. A king was born!

The men packed their bags and
loaded their camels for the trip.
It was going to take
some time. But they
knew the star would
lead them to the new
king. So they followed it.

148

The men stopped at King Herod's palace in Jerusalem. "Where is the king of the Jews who has been born?" they asked.

King Herod was not happy because he did not want another king in his kingdom. He asked the priests and teachers of the law if they knew where this king was.

"The prophet said he would come to Bethlehem," they told King Herod.

The king told the wise men, "Look for the baby in Bethlehem and tell me where you find him."

The wise men continued to follow the star, and it led them to a little house. This was it!

A woman opened the door. And a little toddler peeked out from behind her skirt. The wise men entered, each with a present. They put their gifts at the feet of young Jesus—gold and rich spices. Gifts fit for a king. They had found the Son of God.

The wise men were warned in a dream not to go back to King Herod. So they went home without telling the king where Jesus was.

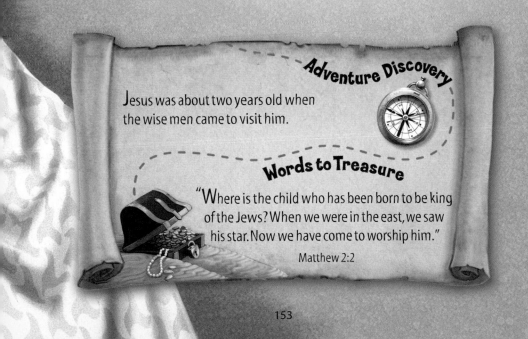

Adventure Discovery

Jesus was about two years old when the wise men came to visit him.

Words to Treasure

"Where is the child who has been born to be king of the Jews? When we were in the east, we saw his star. Now we have come to worship him."

Matthew 2:2

Lost?

Every year Jesus and his family traveled from their home in Nazareth to Jerusalem for the Passover celebration. But this year, on their way home, the festive feeling of the holiday disappeared.

Jesus, who was now twelve years old, was missing. Without wasting another minute, Mary and Joseph hurried back to the city to find their son. But no one had seen him. No one knew where he was.

After three days of searching and worry, Mary rested on a bench outside the temple.

Wait. What was that? Mary knew that voice. It was Jesus! She ran through the entrance of the temple and found him talking with the church leaders. He listened to their questions and gave the answers. The leaders were amazed by his understanding.

Mary ran to Jesus and hugged him. "Where have you been?" she asked. "We were so worried!"

Jesus replied, "Didn't you know I had to be in my Father's house?"

Mary looked at her calm son. She didn't understand everything, but she knew Jesus was special. Someday he would save the world. But right then, she just kissed his forehead and said, "I love you, Jesus." She took his hand, joined Joseph, and headed back to Nazareth, where Jesus learned how to be a carpenter until his ministry began.

Adventure Discovery

A carpenter is someone who builds things out of wood, like chairs and houses.

Words to Treasure

Jesus became wiser and stronger. He also became more and more pleasing to God and to people.

Luke 2:52

Jesus Is Baptized

Matthew 3:13 – 17

The water shimmered and sparkled in the sunlight as the people waded in. John stood in the middle of the river, ready to baptize whoever came to him. When he looked up, he recognized his cousin Jesus.

John shook his head. He said, "I need to be baptized by *you*, Jesus. So why do you come to me?"

"It is right for us to do this," Jesus replied. "It carries out God's holy plan."

So John baptized Jesus, dunking him completely under water, just like the others.

As soon as Jesus came out of the water, the skies opened up.

Jesus saw the Spirit of God coming down on him like a dove.

A voice from heaven said, "This is my Son, and I love him. I am very pleased with him."

Jesus left the river and went into the desert to fast and to pray for forty days.

Adventure Discovery

People are still baptized today. Some are baptized when they are babies. Others are baptized when they are older.

Words to Treasure

"This is my Son, and I love him. I am very pleased with him."

Matthew 3:17

The Devil Tempts Jesus

Matthew 4:1 – 11

The hot sun beat down on the desert—the cactus, the lizards, the sand. Jesus wiped the sweat from his forehead as he prayed. It had been more than one month since Jesus had eaten anything.

Satan knew Jesus was hungry, and he hoped Jesus would be weak. Maybe this would be a good time to trick Jesus into sinning, he thought. So the Devil said to Jesus, "If you are the Son of God, tell these stones to become bread."

Jesus replied, " 'Man doesn't live only on bread. He also lives on every word that comes from the mouth of the Lord' " (Deuteronomy 8:3). Jesus had passed the first test.

Then Jesus stood at the top of the temple. The Devil said, "If you are the Son of God, throw yourself down. It is written, 'The Lord will command his angels to take good care of you.'"

Jesus answered, "It is also written, 'Don't put the Lord your God to the test'" (Deuteronomy 6:16). Jesus had passed the second test.

Then Jesus stood on a very high mountain. The Devil showed him all the kingdoms of the world and their glory. "If you bow down and worship me," Satan said, "I will give you all of this."

Jesus said, "Get away from me, Satan! It is written, 'Worship the Lord your God. He is the only one you should serve'" (Deuteronomy 6:13). Jesus had passed the third test.

The Devil could not trick Jesus. So the Devil left. And angels came and took care of Jesus.

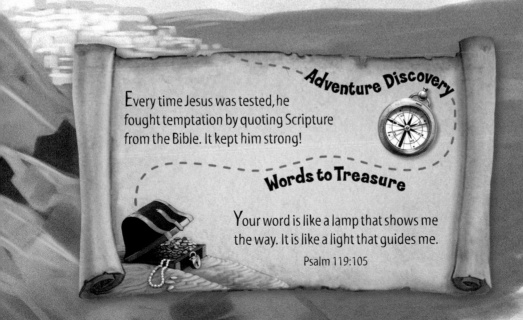

Adventure Discovery

Every time Jesus was tested, he fought temptation by quoting Scripture from the Bible. It kept him strong!

Words to Treasure

Your word is like a lamp that shows me the way. It is like a light that guides me.

Psalm 119:105

Calling the Disciples

Matthew 4:18 – 22

The waves gently rolled onto the beach as Jesus walked along the shore. He scanned the horizon and saw what he was looking for. Two boats bobbed on the waves in the distance with fish nets drifting in the water.

Jesus waved to the fishermen in the boats. "Come. Follow me!" he called.

Jesus' words captured their attention. The fishermen wanted to find out who this person was. When they rowed closer to shore, Jesus said, "I will make you fishers of people."

Now they were really interested. They left their boats and fish nets behind and went with Jesus.

They never imagined they were beginning the biggest adventure of their lives—being disciples of Jesus!

Fishing was a common occupation in Jesus' time. Fishermen on the Sea of Galilee caught different kinds of fish — carp, sardines, and tilapia.

Adventure Discovery

Words to Treasure

"Come. Follow me," Jesus said.

Matthew 4:19

Through the Roof

Mark 2:1 – 12

What was all the commotion? Dozens and dozens of people passed the man as they hurried to a nearby house. They kicked up dust so thick the man started to cough. His cough shook his entire body, causing his lame leg to slip off his mat. He pulled it back with his good arm. Then he lay back down, exhausted.

Another group of people approached—friends of the man. Each one took a corner of his mat. They lifted him up and carried him down the street. One of his friends grinned and said, "We're going to see Jesus, and we're taking you with us."

Crowds of people surrounded the house where Jesus was. So the four friends went up the stairs of the house to the flat roof. Nothing was going to stop them from getting their friend to Jesus.

In a matter of minutes, the man was lowered through a hole in the roof right in front of Jesus.

Jesus looked at the man. Then he looked up at the roof and saw the four friends peering in. Jesus saw their faith. He turned to the man on the mat and said, "Your sins are forgiven. Get up. Take your mat and go home."

The man was astonished. He got up and walked outside where his friends were waiting. They ran down the street together, celebrating this amazing thing Jesus had done!

Adventure Discovery

The roofs on many houses were flat and made of tree branches covered with mud and straw. The branches could easily be removed.

Words to Treasure

They praised God and said, "We have never seen anything like this!"

Mark 2:12

Do Not Worry

Matthew 6:25 – 34

Crowds of people followed Jesus. They wanted to hear him teach. So he went up on a mountainside and sat down. His disciples were there too.

Jesus said to the crowd, "I tell you, do not worry. Don't worry about your life and what you will eat or drink. And don't worry about your body and what you will wear. Isn't there more to life than eating? Aren't there more important things for the body than clothes?

"Look at the birds of the air," said Jesus, pointing to the sky. "They don't plant or gather crops. They don't put away crops in storerooms. But your Father who is in heaven feeds them. Aren't you worth much more than they are?"

Beautiful flowers dotted the hillside. Their delicate petals fluttered in the wind. And they smelled as sweet as perfume.

"And why do you worry about clothes?" said Jesus. "See how the wildflowers grow. They don't work or make clothing."

Then Jesus compared the flowers to King Solomon, Israel's richest king. "Not even Solomon in all of his glory was dressed like one of those flowers," he said. If God dresses the grass of the field so beautifully, won't he dress us even better?

It doesn't help to worry. It won't add "even one hour" of time to our lives. God knows we need food and clothes. And he will give them to us, explained Jesus.

"Put God's kingdom first," said Jesus. "Do what he wants you to do. Then all of those things will also be given to you."

To put "God's kingdom first" means to choose things that would please God above everything else.

Adventure Discovery

Words to Treasure

"I tell you, do not worry."

Matthew 6:25

Treasure!

Matthew 13:44–45

The day was coming to a close, with the setting sun low in the sky. But the man didn't notice because he was so determined to find what he was looking for. He had sold everything to buy this field because he knew it held something special.

Dig, throw, dig, throw. His back ached and his hands throbbed, but he pressed on. *Clank!* went his shovel. "It must be a rock," sighed the man. He kept working. Soon he realized that this was no rock. This was what he had been searching for ... *treasure!*

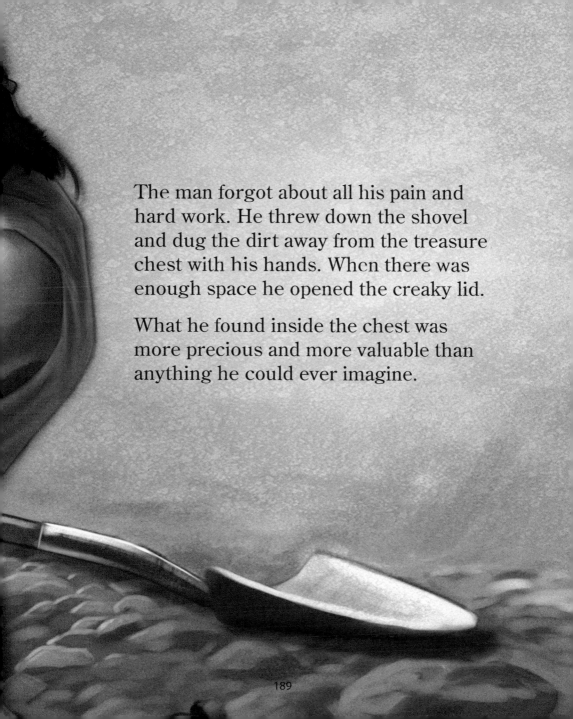

The man forgot about all his pain and
hard work. He threw down the shovel
and dug the dirt away from the treasure
chest with his hands. When there was
enough space he opened the creaky lid.

What he found inside the chest was
more precious and more valuable than
anything he could ever imagine.

Jesus taught the people many things about the kingdom of heaven so they could understand what it was like. He told them this story about finding treasure: "The kingdom of heaven is like treasure that was hidden in a field. When a man found it, he hid it again. He was very happy. So he went and sold everything he had. And he bought that field."

Jesus said that we should search for God like the man searched for the treasure. We need to keep at it, keep pressing on, keep digging deeper to know him, love him, and follow him.

Adventure Discovery

People in ancient times did not have banks. They buried their treasures and money in a field. Sometimes the treasure would not be found for many years.

Words to Treasure

"The kingdom of heaven is like treasure that was hidden in a field."

Matthew 13:44

Stormy Night

Matthew 8:23 – 27

The calm night of sailing across the Sea of Galilee had turned into a stormy disaster. The disciples controlled the boat as best they could, but water was pouring in and they were afraid.

They called out, "Jesus, save us!"

Jesus rubbed his eyes. Just moments ago he had been sleeping in the boat, unaware of the change in the weather.

Frightened, the disciples clung with all their might to the sides of the boat. But not Jesus. He stood up and simply said to the storm, "Be still!"

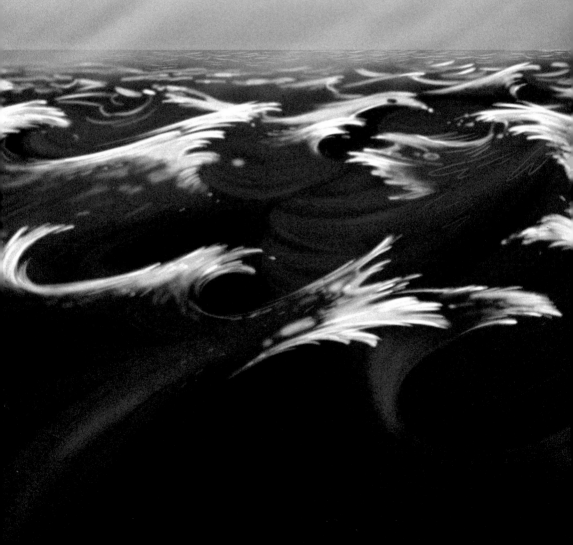

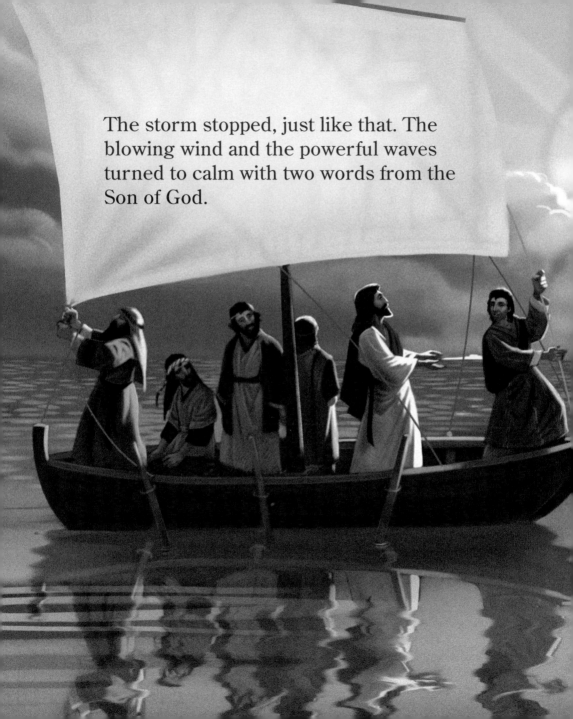

The storm stopped, just like that. The blowing wind and the powerful waves turned to calm with two words from the Son of God.

The disciples turned to each other in relief and amazement. "What kind of man is this? Even the winds and the waves obey him!"

They had never experienced anything like this. And they would never forget.

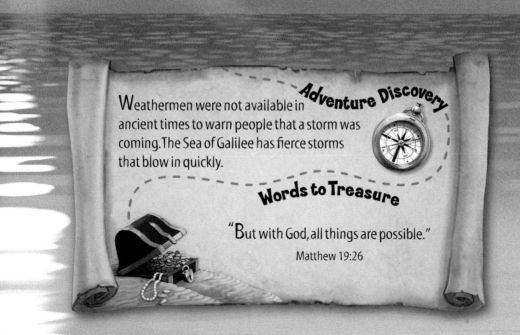

Adventure Discovery

Weathermen were not available in ancient times to warn people that a storm was coming. The Sea of Galilee has fierce storms that blow in quickly.

Words to Treasure

"But with God, all things are possible."

Matthew 19:26

Jesus Heals a Woman

Luke 8:43 – 48

Just a few steps more and she would be in front of Jesus. But too many people stood in the way, and she couldn't push through the crowd. She leaned hard on her cane, and her shoulders slumped. For a moment she thought about turning around and going home.

No! she told herself. Do not give up. Here is
Jesus. He is your only hope. The woman reached
through the crowd of people, stretching, her hand
shaking. Finally she touched his cloak.

Immediately she felt a surge of power go through her. And heal her.

Jesus turned around and asked, "Who touched me?"

The woman fell at his feet and said, "I did. I touched you."

"Good woman," he said, eyes filled with love and tenderness. "Please, get up. Your faith has healed you."

This man Jesus was amazing! He had changed her life. She dropped her cane and walked tall. Today was a new day. All because of Jesus. She was healed!

Adventure Discovery

This very sick woman had been bleeding for twelve years.

Words to Treasure

He said to her, "Dear woman, your faith has healed you. Go in peace. You are free from your suffering."

Mark 5:34

Run for Her Life

Luke 8:40 – 55

Just a little bit farther, the man told himself. His heart was pounding so hard he was afraid it would burst. But all he could think about was his little girl. She was so sick and needed help right away. Just when he felt like he couldn't go any farther, he saw a crowd up ahead.

Jesus turned around as the man approached. "Jesus," the man called out. "Jesus, please help. My daughter is very sick," he said as he bent down to catch his breath.

Just then a messenger came up to the crowd and pulled the man aside. He did not have good news. The little girl had died. Jesus put his hand on the man's shoulder and said, "It's not too late. Your daughter will be healed. Just believe."

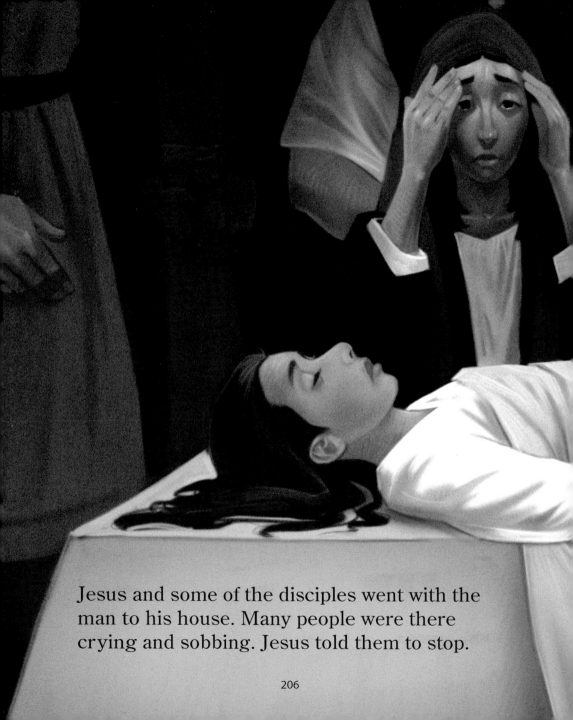

Jesus and some of the disciples went with the
man to his house. Many people were there
crying and sobbing. Jesus told them to stop.

He went to the girl, along with her mom and dad. As she lay very still on her bed, Jesus took her hand. "My child, get up!" he said.

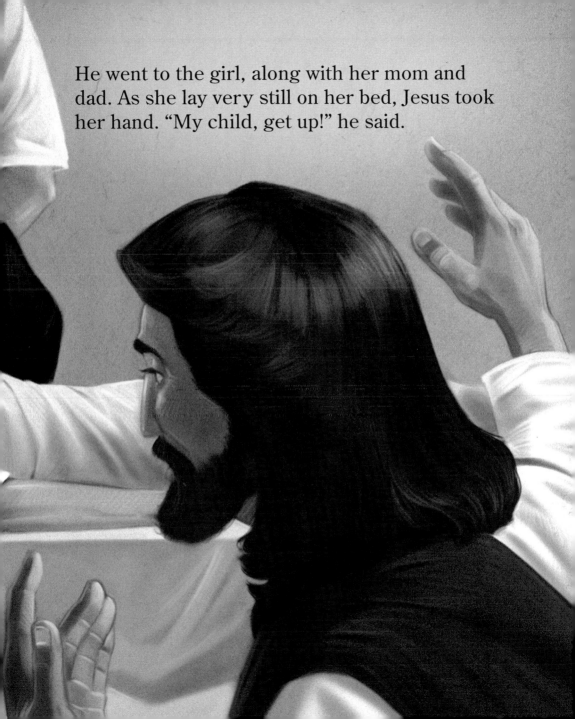

The girl opened her eyes and looked around.
She was alive again!

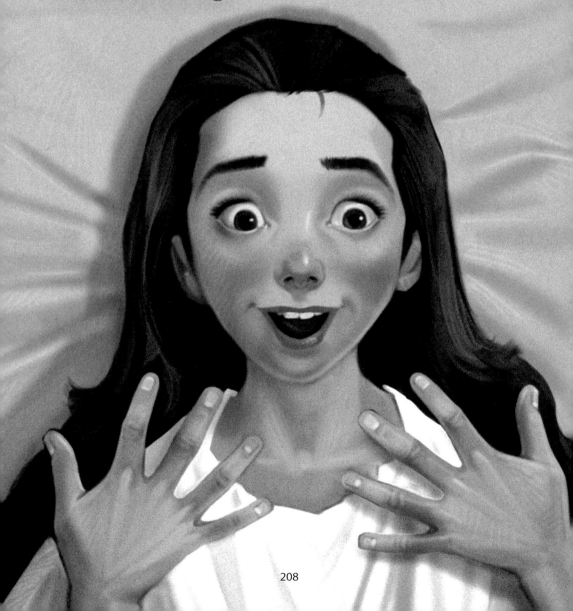

Her dad scooped her up in his arms. He kissed her as happy tears streamed down his face.

Jesus had done the impossible. He had brought the little girl back to life!

Adventure Discovery

The little girl's father was the ruler of the synagogue. He would lead the service, select people to help, and make sure that everyone followed the rules.

Words to Treasure

"Don't be afraid. Just believe. She will be healed."

Luke 8:50

Jesus Heals a Blind Man

John 9:1 – 7

As Jesus walked down the road, he noticed a blind man. The man had been blind since he was born. The man had never seen the faces of his mother and father. He had never seen trees or grass or flowers. He had never seen the sun, moon, and stars. His eyes just didn't work.

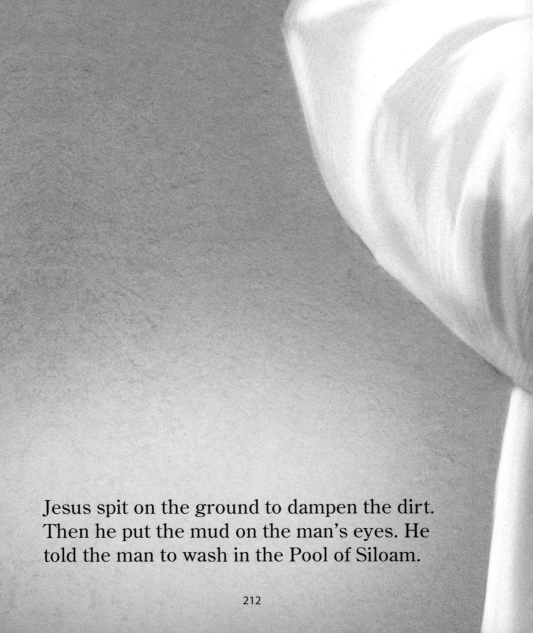

Jesus spit on the ground to dampen the dirt.
Then he put the mud on the man's eyes. He
told the man to wash in the Pool of Siloam.

So the man did as Jesus said. As the water washed away the mud, something began to happen. Light began to filter through the darkness. Slowly the man opened his eyes. He looked around in amazement at the trees and flowers, people and animals. How wonderful to go home and finally see the faces of his parents. How surprised and thankful to Jesus they all must have been!

The Pool of Siloam was cut out of rocks. The water in it was considered sacred. The pool is still in Jerusalem today.

Words to Treasure

"I am the light of the world."
John 9:5

The Lost Son

Luke 15:11 – 24

What a very unusual place to find someone. There, in a muddy field surrounded by pigs, sat a filthy man. His torn clothes and tangled hair smelled like the dirty animals.

His stomach ached with hunger. He hadn't eaten in days. Even the pig slop looked good to him. He wondered, How had life come to this?

The man remembered when he had been back
home with his father and his brother. There
had always been food on the table. He had
never been hungry. He had always worn nice
clothes, and he knew his father loved him. But
still he had been determined to leave home.

He had wanted to see other places, so he had boldly demanded that his father give him his inheritance money.

At first everything turned out better than he imagined. His bag of money overflowed, and he made a lot of friends. He bought them meals and drinks and even fancy hats and sparkly rings! But as soon as his money ran out, his friends did too. Not one person stayed with him.

So the man left the city and found the best job he could, feeding pigs at a farm. And there he sat in the mud with the smelly animals.

A thought struck him. My father has plenty of servants working for him who are treated well and have good food to eat. I know I've done many bad things, but maybe my father will forgive me and let me be one of his servants.

The man got up from the pigpen and walked home. Before he even reached his house, he saw someone running down the road toward him. It was his father!

They hugged for a long time, and tears streamed down their faces. The father was so glad to see that his son had come home. He not only welcomed his son back, he dressed him with the best robe and celebrated with a huge party!

When we do something wrong, Jesus forgives us with this same kind of love.

Adventure Discovery

Feeding pigs was the worst kind of work for a Jewish person. They viewed pigs as "unclean" animals and tried to have nothing to do with them.

Words to Treasure

"While the son was still a long way off, his father saw him. He was filled with tender love for his son. He ran to him. He threw his arms around him and kissed him."

Luke 15:20

Lazarus Lives!

John 11:1–44

Jesus stood at the entrance of the tomb and called, "Come out!"

Like an old scary movie, a mummy walked out of the tomb, its cloth bandages starting to unravel.

Mary and Martha couldn't believe it. Four days earlier their brother had died, and they had placed him in this tomb. Now someone was walking out! Surely this couldn't be real.

The sisters held their breath. The bandages fell off. It was ...

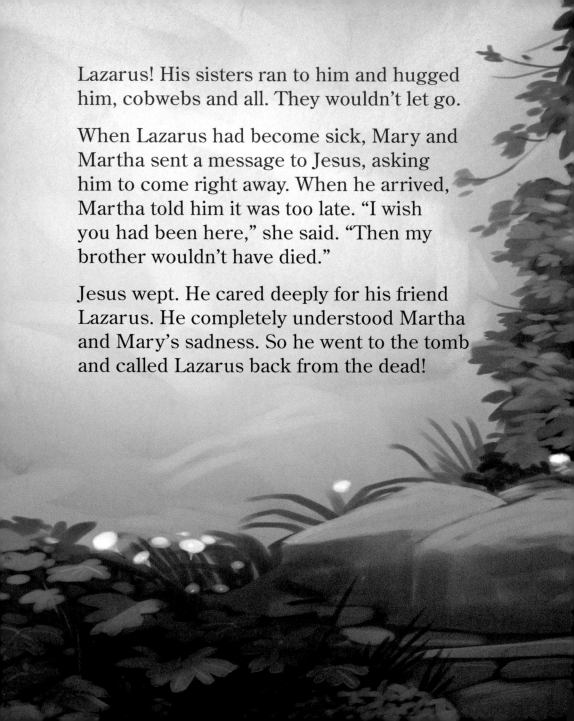

Lazarus! His sisters ran to him and hugged him, cobwebs and all. They wouldn't let go.

When Lazarus had become sick, Mary and Martha sent a message to Jesus, asking him to come right away. When he arrived, Martha told him it was too late. "I wish you had been here," she said. "Then my brother wouldn't have died."

Jesus wept. He cared deeply for his friend Lazarus. He completely understood Martha and Mary's sadness. So he went to the tomb and called Lazarus back from the dead!

That night, Jesus sat around the dinner table
with Mary, Martha, and Lazarus. They
treasured every minute and were so happy to
be together again.

Jesus has feelings just like we do. When we are sad, he is sad. He understands our pain and he cares about us.

Adventure Discovery

Words to Treasure

Jesus sobbed.

John 11:35

Jesus and the Kids

Matthew 19:13 – 15

On a warm, sunny day, a group of children laughed and played tag. "You're it!" a girl giggled as she ran out of reach. A boy hid behind a tree. And the game went on.

Jesus smiled at their gentle hearts, tender spirits, and fearless wonder. Oh, how he loved children. Not just these children but all the children in the whole world.

Just then their mothers called out, "Come here! Let's talk to Jesus and ask him to pray for you."

But the disciples stood in their way. "Don't bother Jesus. He's too busy," they said.

Jesus didn't agree. "Let the children come to me," he called out to the disciples. "Do not keep them away."

The children joyfully ran to Jesus, laughing and giggling.

He lifted them onto his lap and smiled at them. He laughed with them and gave them hugs.

Adventure Discovery

What a friend we have in Jesus!

Words to Treasure

Jesus said, "Let the little children come to me. Don't keep them away. The kingdom of heaven belongs to people like them."

Matthew 19:14

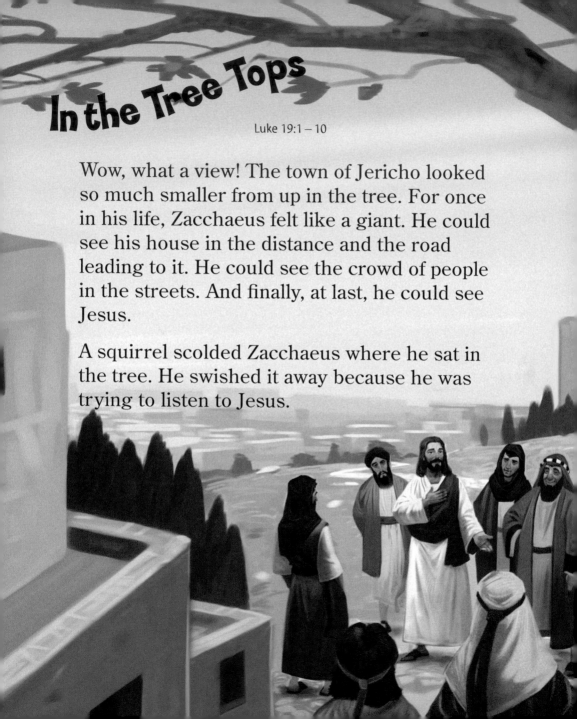

In the Tree Tops

Luke 19:1 – 10

Wow, what a view! The town of Jericho looked so much smaller from up in the tree. For once in his life, Zacchaeus felt like a giant. He could see his house in the distance and the road leading to it. He could see the crowd of people in the streets. And finally, at last, he could see Jesus.

A squirrel scolded Zacchaeus where he sat in the tree. He swished it away because he was trying to listen to Jesus.

As Zacchaeus sat quietly, Jesus looked up into the tree. In front of the crowd of people, Jesus called his name. "Zacchaeus, come down from that tree. I'm going to your house today," he said.

Zacchaeus scrambled down the branches and trunk. As he scurried through the crowd, the people booed at the short man. It was no secret that Zacchaeus was a tax collector and had cheated many of his neighbors out of money.

But Jesus didn't boo. Instead, he smiled and motioned for Zacchaeus to walk with him. Soon they reached Zacchaeus' house and went inside.

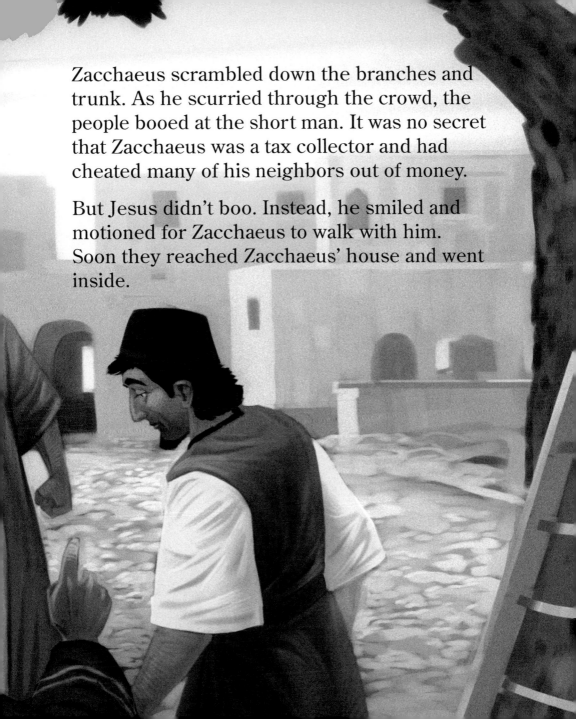

By the end of their time together, Zacchaeus' life was changed. He promised Jesus he would stop his bad ways and pay people back four times the amount of money he had stolen from them.

As Zacchaeus waved good-bye, he felt thankful for Jesus' visit. He took out his money and started counting it—to see how much he needed to return. Through his window he could see the big tree ... and he grinned.

Adventure Discovery

Tax collectors collected money from the people for the government. But many tax collectors took more money than was needed, so they could keep some for themselves.

Words to Treasure

Put up with each other. Forgive the things you are holding against one another. Forgive, just as the Lord forgave you.

Colossians 3:13

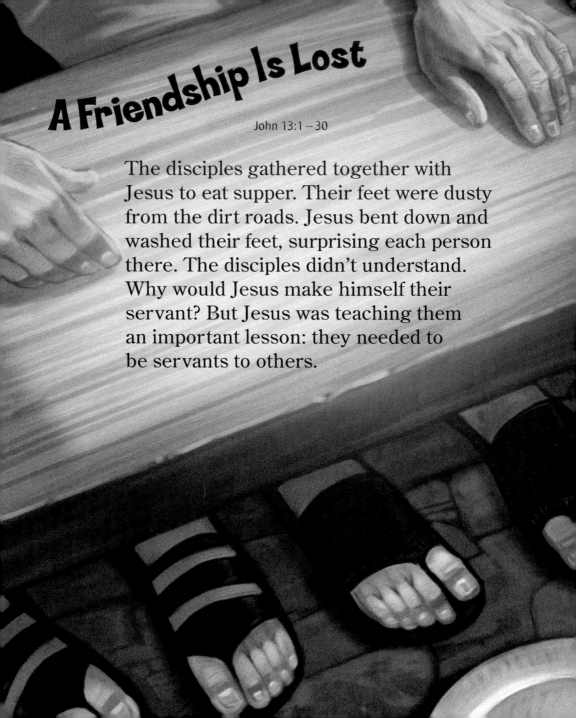

A Friendship Is Lost

John 13:1 – 30

The disciples gathered together with Jesus to eat supper. Their feet were dusty from the dirt roads. Jesus bent down and washed their feet, surprising each person there. The disciples didn't understand. Why would Jesus make himself their servant? But Jesus was teaching them an important lesson: they needed to be servants to others.

As the sun was setting, the disciples sat at the table. Jesus locked eyes with Judas. Then he turned to the rest of them. Jesus broke the bread on his plate and said, "This is my body, given for you." Then he poured wine into his cup and said, "This is my blood, shed for you."

As they finished supper, Jesus motioned for them to pay attention to him. "One of you will betray me this very night," said Jesus. The disciples looked at each other in disbelief.

"Surely, it isn't me?" one person said. "Jesus, is it me?" asked another. In the midst of the questions, Jesus again locked eyes with Judas.

Then Judas slipped out the back door into the night.

Adventure Discovery

Judas received thirty pieces of silver for telling the enemy where Jesus was.

Words to Treasure

A worthless and evil man goes around saying twisted things with his mouth....Trouble will catch up with him in an instant.

Proverbs 6:12,15

Jesus Is Captured

Matthew 26:36 – 46

After the disciples were finished eating supper, a few of them walked with Jesus to a garden called Gethsemane. This was one of Jesus' favorite places to pray. "Stay. Sit here while I go over there to pray," he said to them.

Jesus walked over to a group of trees, knelt on the ground, and began to pray to God, his Father.

Jesus knew that his time on earth was coming to an end. He thought about all the people he had met and how much he loved them.

Jesus prayed, "Father, take this suffering from me. But if it is your will, then I will accept that too."

His body shook. Sweat poured down his face as he prayed about the trouble that was coming.

Jesus got up and walked back to the disciples. They were sleeping. Jesus sighed. He would have to face his suffering alone.

Then he saw torches coming in the distance.

Adventure Discovery

The garden of Gethsemane is located on a hill called the Mount of Olives. The garden had many olive trees in it when Jesus was alive.

Words to Treasure

"My Father, if it is possible, take this cup of suffering away from me. But let what you want be done, not what I want."

Matthew 26:39

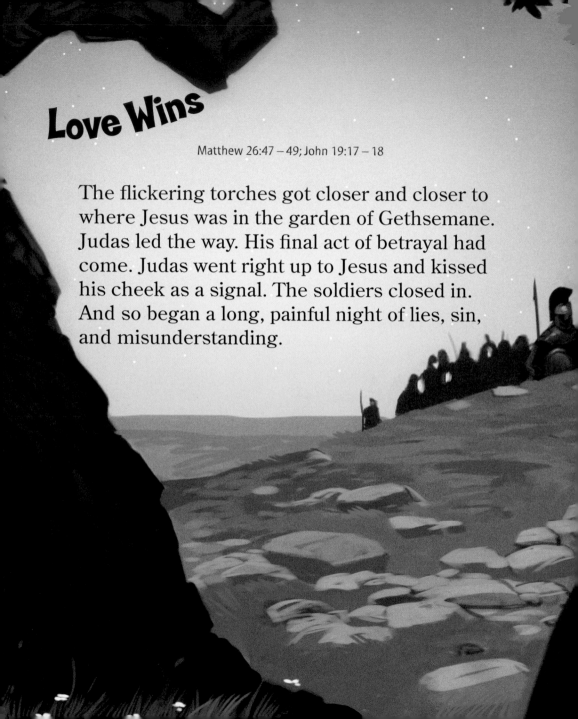

Love Wins

Matthew 26:47 – 49; John 19:17 – 18

The flickering torches got closer and closer to where Jesus was in the garden of Gethsemane. Judas led the way. His final act of betrayal had come. Judas went right up to Jesus and kissed his cheek as a signal. The soldiers closed in. And so began a long, painful night of lies, sin, and misunderstanding.

On the walk to Golgotha, "the place of the skull," Jesus carried a heavy, wooden cross on his bleeding back. Each step was a painful struggle.

Then Roman soldiers nailed Jesus to the cross. And in a few hours, Jesus died. For you. For me. For the whole world.

In the greatest act of love we will ever know, Jesus took our sins away. He paid for them on the cross. And now, if we believe he is our Savior, we can live with him forever in heaven someday.

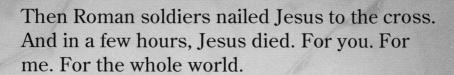

Adventure Discovery

Jesus died in the middle of the afternoon. But it became as dark as night for three hours, and an earthquake shook the ground.

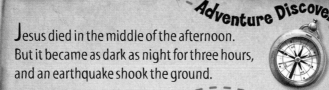

Words to Treasure

But here is how God has shown his love for us. While we were still sinners, Christ died for us.

Romans 5:8

Jesus Is Alive!

Mark 16:1 – 11

The tomb was empty! How could it be? The huge stone had been rolled away from the entrance. Mary Magdalene, Salome, and Mary, the mother of James, had brought spices with them to put on Jesus' body.

But his body wasn't there!

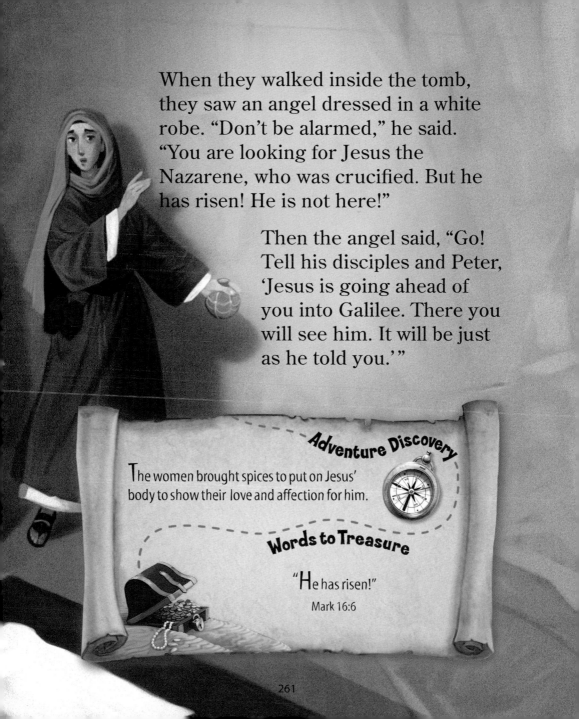

When they walked inside the tomb, they saw an angel dressed in a white robe. "Don't be alarmed," he said. "You are looking for Jesus the Nazarene, who was crucified. But he has risen! He is not here!"

Then the angel said, "Go! Tell his disciples and Peter, 'Jesus is going ahead of you into Galilee. There you will see him. It will be just as he told you.'"

Adventure Discovery

The women brought spices to put on Jesus' body to show their love and affection for him.

Words to Treasure

"He has risen!"

Mark 16:6

Heaven Bound

Acts 1:1 – 11

After his suffering and death, Jesus appeared to his disciples for forty days. They were a little scared, surprised, and happy all at the same time. Jesus proved that he was alive again by eating with them and showing them scars from the nails in his hands.

While Jesus was with them, he continued to tell them about God's kingdom. One day he said, "Wait in Jerusalem for the gift my Father promised. You have heard me talk about it. John baptized with water. But in a few days you will be baptized with the Holy Spirit. Once you receive the power of the Holy Spirit, you will be my witnesses to the whole world by telling them about me."

Then as the disciples watched, Jesus was taken up to heaven. Soon a cloud hid Jesus from their sight.

Suddenly two men dressed in white clothes appeared next to the disciples. "Men of Galilee," they said, "why do you stand here looking at the sky? Jesus has been taken away into heaven. But he will come back."

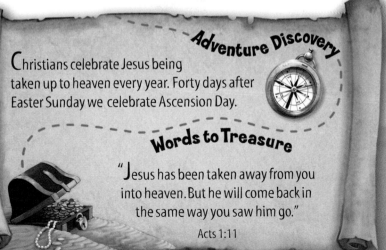

Adventure Discovery

Christians celebrate Jesus being taken up to heaven every year. Forty days after Easter Sunday we celebrate Ascension Day.

Words to Treasure

"Jesus has been taken away from you into heaven. But he will come back in the same way you saw him go."

Acts 1:11

Spirit Fire

Acts 2:1 – 41

The disciples gathered in a house in Jerusalem, like Jesus had told them to do before he was taken to heaven. Suddenly, surprisingly, a rushing, whirling wind started to blow *inside* the house!

Something that looked like tongues of fire settled on each person in the room. But it didn't burn them or hurt them. They were filled with the Holy Spirit and were given the power to speak in languages they had not known before.

Jewish people from every country in the world were staying in the city of Jerusalem. When they heard the men of Galilee speaking in their own languages, they were amazed and confused.

Peter explained to them that the Holy Spirit had come. It was just as the great prophet Joel had predicted. Peter quoted the Bible saying, "Everyone who calls out to me will be saved" (Joel 2:32).

Peter continued, "So be sure of this, all you people of Israel. You nailed Jesus to the cross. But God has made him both Lord and Christ."

When the people heard this, they felt ashamed. They asked Peter and the other apostles, "What should we do?"

Peter replied, "Turn away from your sins and be baptized in the name of Jesus Christ. Then your sins will be forgiven. You will receive the gift of the Holy Spirit."

About three thousand people joined the believers that day!

Adventure Discovery

The Holy Spirit is part of the Holy Trinity of God — the Father, the Son, and the Holy Spirit.

Words to Treasure

All of them were filled with the Holy Spirit.

Acts 2:4

Jail Quake

Acts 16:16—40

Paul and Silas weren't ordinary men. Even in the middle of the night while they sat in jail, they did an extraordinary thing—they prayed and sang songs to God. As other prisoners listened, their voices echoed against the cold stone walls. Their feet were in chains. They had been cruelly beaten and whipped. But still, they chose to praise and worship God.

Suddenly a great noise filled the halls of the prison. The floor began to shake. The jail bars rattled. Everyone's chains came loose. And the prison doors flew open! For the prisoners, the earthquake was their chance to get away!

The guard thought everyone had escaped. He trembled with fear because he would be punished if he didn't do his job. But Paul called out to him, "Don't worry. We are all here!"

Scared and amazed, the jailer rushed into the cell. He fell down at the feet of Paul and Silas and asked, "What must I do to be saved?"

They replied, "Believe in the Lord Jesus."

The jailer took Paul and Silas to his house
where he and his whole family were baptized.
Their lives were changed forever, and they
were filled with incredible joy.

The next morning, Paul and Silas were set free. They traveled to other places in order to tell more people about Jesus.

Adventure Discovery

Paul and Silas were punished and thrown into jail because they had helped a slave girl.

Words to Treasure

"Believe in the Lord Jesus. Then you and your family will be saved."

Acts 16:31

Shipwrecked!

Acts 27:13 — 28:10

Paul clung to a chunk of wood as he drifted ashore. The battered ship he had been sailing on crashed against the rocks near the Island of Malta. Thankful to be alive, Paul crawled onto the beach.

By God's mercy all 276 men survived the shipwreck. It was just as the angel had told Paul: "Do not be afraid, Paul ... God has shown his grace by sparing the lives of all those sailing with you."

It was cold and raining, so the men made a campfire. As Paul added more sticks to the fire, a snake darted out and bit Paul's hand!

He flicked the deadly snake off his arm, but the native people watched and worried. How long until Paul started to swell up and suffer from the poison?

Miraculously Paul was fine. Nothing happened to him. The people were amazed.

During the three months that Paul stayed with the people of Malta, he healed them of their sicknesses and diseases. And he told them about Jesus and what it means to be a Christian.

The poisonous snake that bit Paul was a viper. But snakes no longer live on the island of Malta.

Adventure Discovery

Words to Treasure

"I belong to God and serve him."

Acts 27:23

The Journeys of Paul

Paul traveled to many places.
Everywhere he went, he told
people about Jesus. He helped
spread the news of
Jesus our Savior
throughout the world.

Rome

Syracuse

Philippi

Thessalonica

Antioch

Lystra

Ephesus

Derbe

Athens

Attalia

Tarsus

Corinth

Salamis

Paphos

Antioch

Tyre

Caesarea

Jerusalem

The Adventure Continues...

So ends our journey through some of the stories in the Bible. We've had many adventures along the way, from creation to Jonah to Jesus to Paul and his work spreading the news of Jesus around the world.

But the adventure isn't over. The most important thing has yet to happen ... Jesus is coming back!

Here are some clues from the Bible about Jesus' return to earth from heaven:

1 Thessalonians 4:1–17	Jesus will return someday to take his followers home.
Acts 1:11	Jesus will return the same way he left.
Luke 21:8	Many will pretend to be like Jesus and mislead a lot of people.
Revelation 20:10	Satan will be punished and defeated; Satan will not win, God will.
Luke 21:34–36	Jesus will come at a time when we do not expect. So we need to be ready.
Matthew 28:18–20	Jesus calls us to continue the work he started until he returns.
John 20:21	Again Jesus said, "May peace be with you! The Father has sent me. So now I am sending you."

Words to Treasure

But the Lord is faithful. He will strengthen you.
He will guard you from the evil one.

2 Thessalonians 3:3

Check out the entire Adventure Bible Family

A journey of faith begins with the first step. From preschoolers to pre-teens, the *Adventure Bible* helps kids find their way.

For Kids 6-9

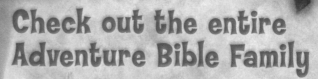

Designed especially for early readers who are ready to explore the Bible on their own.

9780310715474

This yearlong devotional takes children on a thrilling journey of spiritual growth and discovery.

9780310714484

For Kids 9-12

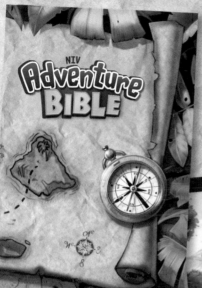

Filled with great adventures and exciting features, this #1 Bible for kids opens a fresh new encounter with God's Word.

9780310715436

365 Days of Adventure

NIV Adventure Bible Book of Devotions

A full year's worth of daily devotions for kids that will capture their imagination, teach them about God, and help them live a life of faith.

9780310714477

written by Robin Schmitt

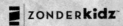